RECIPES FOR ONE
for a healthier you!

Your Creative Kitchen®
from www.rosemaryconley.com

First published in 2019 by Digital Wellbeing Limited.

www.digitalwellbeing.co

Recipes created by Sarah Skelton
Designed by Alice Brown
Edited by Tori Perrot
Production director: Sarah Skelton

Publisher: Independent Publishing Network.
Publication date: 2019
ISBN: 9781789721737
Email: info@digitalwellbeing.co
Address: Digital Wellbeing Limited, Vanquish House, Wellesley Road, Tharston, Norfolk, NR15 2PD
Website: www.rosemaryconley.com
Printed in United Kingdom

Publisher's notes
While every care has been taken in compiling the recipes for this book, Digital Wellbeing Limited, or any other persons who have been involved in working on this publication, cannot accept responsibility for any errors or omissions, inadvertent or not, that may be found in the recipes or text, not for any problems that may arise as a result of preparing one of these recipes. If you are pregnant or breastfeeding or have any special dietary requirements or medical conditions, it is advisable to consult a medical professional before following any of the recipes contained in this book.

Dear Reader,

Welcome to Recipes for One!

So many cookbooks offer recipes for four but if you are someone who lives alone that can be frustrating. In this cookbook, over 80 recipes have been specially created for anyone cooking for one, which can also be doubled-up if you wish to cook for more than just you.

This beautiful full-colour cookbook proves just how easy it is to prepare healthy, delicious food in minutes. With all the nutritional information included for each recipe, and clear instructions as to how to prepare it, you can make educated choices to suit your individual taste and health requirements. And if you are watching your waistline, the number of calories are included in each recipe too.

We all want to prepare and eat healthy meals with the minimum of fuss and effort. All of the recipes in this book have been created by my friend and colleague Sarah Skelton. Sarah is CEO of Rosemary Online, our online weight-loss club at www.rosemaryconley.com. If you go to our website you will be able to see Sarah preparing an assortment of dishes in the Your Creative Kitchen section.

Sarah and I have worked together for over 20 years and as well as being qualified to teach exercise and nutrition, she is a highly accomplished and greatly respected cook. Not only does Sarah create many healthy recipes for our website, she also created the recipes for my book *The 3-2-1 Diet.* Sarah is unquestionably a master in the kitchen and has a real skill in combining exciting tastes with healthy eating. I am sure you will love what she has created for you.

In this book Sarah will inspire you with an array of different flavours and dishes, including main meals, lunches, soups, sides and sauces, as well as offering lots of useful cooking tips. I am sure you will find the recipes fun to make and delicious to eat. Enjoy!

Very best wishes,

Rosemary Conley CBE

Contents

Fish & Shellfish

Fish Soup

per serving:
Calories 165, Fat 0.8g, Sugar 10g, Salt 1.7g
Prep time: 5 minutes
Cook time: 20 minutes

- **2 spring onions, cleaned, root removed and sliced**
- **200g tomato passata**
- **120ml chicken stock**
- **120g frozen mixed seafood, defrosted, and fish cut into chunks**
- **1 tsp fresh parsley, chopped**
- **½ tsp garlic paste, or 1 small garlic clove, peeled and finely diced**
- **½ tsp smoked paprika**
- **black pepper**
- **rapeseed oil spray**

1. Heat a saucepan over a medium heat and add a couple of sprays of the rapeseed oil. Add the spring onion, garlic paste and paprika and cook for 2-3 minutes stirring occasionally, then pour in the tomato passata and chicken stock. Season with a little black pepper. Bring to the boil, then reduce to a simmer for 6-7 minutes.

2. Add the fish chunks and seafood and continue cooking for 5-6 mins, stir in the parsley.

3. Pour the soup into a warmed bowl and serve straight away.

King Prawn Dhansak Curry

per serving:
Calories 333, Fat 5.2g, Sugar 11g, Salt 2g
Prep time: 5 minutes
Cook time: 25 minutes

- **160g king prawns, raw, peeled and deveined**
- **½ of a 400g can of lentil soup**
- **1 small onion, finely diced**
- **1 x 200g tin of chopped tomatoes**
- **1 small clove of garlic, peeled and finely diced**
- **1½ tsp garam masala or curry powder**
- **½ tsp turmeric**
- **1 small red chilli, deseeded and finely diced or ⅓ tsp of dried chilli flakes**
- **few fresh coriander leaves to serve**
- **rapeseed oil spray**
- **black pepper**

1. Heat a heavy based large saucepan and add a couple of sprays of the rapeseed oil. Add the onion, garlic and chilli and cook gently until softened – about 2-3 minutes.

2. Add the garam masala, turmeric, tomatoes and lentil soup. Stir and reduce to a simmer, then cook for a further 10-15 minutes until the sauce has thickened.

3. Add the raw prawns and gently stir to combine. Cook for a further 5 minutes until the prawns have turned pink.

4. Serve in a warmed bowl topped with freshly ground black pepper and the fresh coriander leaves.

5. Delicious with rice or naan bread or even poured over a jacket potato.

Salmon and Spinach Gnocchi

per serving:
Calories 566, Fat 22g, Sugar 1g, Salt 1.7g
Prep time: 5 minutes
Cook time: 20 minutes

- **130g salmon fillet**
- **150g fresh gnocchi**
- **500ml vegetable stock**
- **1 spring onion, cleaned and sliced**
- **1 small clove of garlic, peeled, and finely diced**
- **1 large handful of washed spinach leaves**
- **rapeseed oil**
- **freshly ground red and black peppercorns**
- **a couple of basil leaves to serve**

1. Heat a non-stick frying pan and add a couple of sprays of the rapeseed oil. Add the spring onion and garlic and cook on a low heat to soften for 2-3 minutes.

2. Remove the skin from the salmon fillet and cut the flesh into 1cm cubes. Add the salmon to the spring onions and garlic and increase the heat slightly. Gently turn the salmon occasionally so not to break up the cubes. After about 3-4 minutes, add the spinach leaves and black and red pepper and turn down the heat, stirring occasionally.

3. Place the vegetable stock into a medium saucepan and bring to the boil. Add the gnocchi and simmer for 1-2 minutes until the dumplings rise to the surface. Drain and add to the salmon and spinach mix. Gently stir so the gnocchi is covered in the salmon juices.

4. Serve straight away, and sprinkle a few basil leaves over the top.

Scallop Risotto

per serving:
Calories 508, Fat 6.0g, Sugar 5.1g, Salt 1.9g
Prep time: 5 minutes
Cook time: 25-30 minutes

- **4 king scallops**
- **200ml hot chicken or vegetable stock**
- **55g (dry weight) Arborio rice**
- **1 small onion, peeled and finely diced**
- **½ tsp garlic paste or 1 small garlic clove peeled and finely diced**
- **1 tomato, deseeded and diced**
- **zest and juice of 1 lemon**
- **salt and pepper to season**
- **a few basil leaves**
- **rapeseed oil spray**

1. Heat a medium saucepan over medium-high heat. Add a couple of sprays of the rapeseed oil, onion and garlic; cook, stirring often, until soft, about 2-4 minutes. Stir in rice and cook, stirring until coated in the onions and garlic for 1-2 minutes.

2. Add a third of the stock and a pinch of salt and a little black pepper. Cook, stirring occasionally (so the rice does not stick to the pan) until almost absorbed. Add the chopped tomato and cook for a further minute.

3. Continue adding the remaining warm stock, about one third at a time, stirring constantly until most of the liquid has been absorbed between additions. The rice should have a creamy consistency, but not mushy.

4. Finely chop one of the basil leaves and add to the rice with the lemon juice and zest, stir gently, then set aside and keep warm.

5. Heat a small frying pan until hot and add a couple of sprays of the rapeseed oil. Season the scallops with a little salt.

6. Place the scallops in the frying pan, and press down gently to ensure they seal properly. Cook for 1-2 minutes on each side or until a golden brown colour.

7. Spoon the warm risotto on to the middle of a warm plate, top with the scallops and remaining basil leaves. Serve straight away.

TIP
If you don't like scallops, why not swap them for 150g of cod fillet (skin removed) and cut into small cubes.
NB you may need to cook the fish for a minute or so longer.

Keralan Style Fish Curry

per serving:
Calories 226, Fat 3.4g, Sugar 18g, Salt 0.75g
Prep time: 10 minutes
Cook time: 15 minutes

- **140g firm white fish, boned and skin removed**
- **1 small red pepper, deseeded and diced**
- **1 small red chilli, deseeded and finely diced**
- **1 clove of garlic, peeled and finely chopped**
- **½ tsp ground turmeric**
- **1 tbsp curry powder**
- **½ tsp mustard seeds**
- **2cm piece of fresh ginger root, peeled and grated**
- **1 small onion, peeled and chopped**
- **1 x 200g can of chopped tomatoes**
- **100ml coconut milk**
- **1 tbsp fresh coriander, to serve (optional)**
- **rapeseed oil spray**

1. Cut the fish into chunks.

2. Heat a large frying pan and add a couple of sprays of the rapeseed oil, then add the mustard seeds and chopped red pepper and cook for 1-2 minutes.

3. Add the onion, garlic, grated ginger and chilli and cook for a further 2 minutes, then add the curry powder and turmeric. Stir to combine the spices.

4. Add the coconut milk and chopped tomatoes. Bring to the boil for 1 minute and then reduce the heat to a simmer. Add the fish and cook for a further 15 minutes until the fish has cooked and the sauce has thickened.

5. Add the fresh coriander and serve straight away.

Spicy Prawn and Courgette Rice

per serving:
Calories 309, Fat 1.8g, Sugar 3.5g, Salt 2g
Prep time: 5 minutes
Cook time: 20 minutes

- **1 tsp tomato puree**
- **120g cooked king prawns**
- **55g (dry weight) basmati and wild rice mix or plain basmati rice**
- **1 medium courgette, cut into quarters, then cut into chunks about 1cm thick**
- **½ tsp chilli flakes**
- **salt and freshly ground black pepper**
- **rapeseed oil spray**

1. Heat a pan of water until boiling and add the rice, wild rice (if using) and chilli flakes. Cook for 15 minutes or until it has fully cooked. Once cooked drain the rice, but keep 2-3 tablespoons of the cooking liquid in reserve.

2. Heat a frying pan and add a couple of sprays of rapeseed oil and add the chopped courgette. Cook for 3-5 minutes until they are starting to soften.

3. Add the rice, reserved cooking liquid, tomato puree and prawns to the frying pan. Reduce the heat slightly and stir all of the ingredients together. Cook for a further 2-3 minutes until the prawns are hot and the cooking liquid has been absorbed. Season with a little salt and pepper and add a few extra chilli flakes if you want to increase the spice. Serve immediately.

Quick and Simple Fish Curry

per serving:
Calories 203, Fat 4.2g, Sugar 11g, Salt 0.8g
Prep time: 5 minutes
Cook time: 20 minutes

- **150g white fish, cut into chunks**
- **150ml coconut milk**
- **1 small onion, peeled and diced**
- **2 tsp garam masala or curry powder**
- **1 small green chilli, deseeded and diced**
- **½ tsp turmeric**
- **½ tsp fennel seeds**
- **½ tsp ground cumin**
- **½ tsp garlic paste or 1 small clove of garlic, peeled and finely diced**

1. Heat a non-stick frying pan to a medium heat.

2. Add the onion, chilli (keep a little back for serving) and garlic and cook gently until softened, 2-3 minutes. Add the garam masala, turmeric, fennel seeds and ground cumin. Cook for a further couple of minutes.

3. Add the coconut milk and reduce the heat to a simmer for 3-4 minutes. Add the fish chunks and cook for a further 5-10 minutes until tender, stirring occasionally.

4. Serve straight away with the remaining chilli sprinkled on top. Great with rice or naan bread.

Luxury Fish Burger

per serving;
Calories 345, Fat 7.6g, Sugar 7.5g, Salt 2.6g
Prep time: 10 minutes
Cook time: 15 minutes

- **140g thick fillet of boned white fish, such as cod or hake**
- **1 brioche roll**
- **½ tsp capers, roughly chopped**
- **juice of half a lemon**
- **1 tbsp lighter than light mayonnaise**
- **rapeseed oil spray**
- **freshly ground red peppercorns**
- **a few mixed salad leaves**
- **a few slices of cucumber or pickled gherkin**

1. Preheat the oven to 200°C, 400°F, Gas Mark 6.

2. Place a piece of baking parchment onto a small baking tray. Place the fish fillet on the tray and spray with a little rapeseed oil. Place the fish in the oven to cook for 10-15 minutes.

3. To make the caper sauce, place the chopped capers, mayonnaise and lemon juice into a small bowl and mix until combined, then set aside.

4. Three minutes before the fish is cooked, slice the brioche roll in half and place cut side up on a baking tray in the oven to crisp slightly. This should take about 3 minutes.

5. Remove the fish and the brioche roll from the oven. Sprinkle the baked fish with some freshly ground red peppercorns.

6. To serve, place the flatter half of the roll on a plate and top with some salad leaves. Place the cooked fish on top and then layer on top the sliced cucumber (or sliced gherkins if you prefer) and a few more salad leaves. Top with the caper sauce and place the other half of the brioche roll on top. Eat straight away.

Pan Fried Cod

with Porcini Mushrooms and Asparagus

per serving:
Calories 203, Fat 4.2g, Sugar 11g, Salt 0.8g
Prep time: 5 minutes
Cook time: 15-20 minutes

- **140g boneless fresh cod fillet**
- **2 fresh porcini mushrooms**
- **80g fresh baby asparagus**
- **pinch of sea salt**
- **black pepper**
- **rapeseed oil**
- **juice of 1 lime**

1. Thinly slice the mushrooms, and trim the woody ends of the asparagus.

2. Heat a non-stick frying pan and add a couple of sprays of rapeseed oil, add the mushrooms and cook for 2-3 minutes, then add the baby asparagus and cook for a further 3-4 minutes. Transfer the cooked mushrooms and asparagus to a warm plate and keep hot.

3. Season the fish with the sea salt and pepper.

4. Re-heat the frying pan again until hot and add the fish skin side down, cook for 3-4 minutes until the skin has started to crisp. Spray the top of the fish with one squirt of the rapeseed oil and turn over, flesh side down. Cook for a further 3-4 minutes until the cod is opaque.

5. Place the mushrooms and asparagus on a warmed serving plate, top with the fish, skin side down, drizzle over the lime juice and serve with pea shoots and fresh fennel fronds (optional).

Ginger Prawn Stir-fry

per serving;
Calories 285, Fat 11g, Sugar 10g, Salt 4.5g
Prep time: 10 minutes
Cook time: 15minutes

- **150g uncooked peeled prawns**
- **160g fresh vegetable and beansprout stir-fry mix**
- **1 small red chilli, deseeded and diced**
- **1 x1½cm cube of ginger, finely grated**
- **2 tsp dark soy sauce**
- **½ tsp sesame oil**

1. Place everything except the vegetable and beansprout stir-fry mix into a small bowl and mix to combine.

2. Heat a large frying pan to hot, add the sesame oil and the prawn marinade mix. Fry for 2-3 minutes until the prawns have started to turn pink.

3. Add the vegetables and continue cooking for a further 3-4 minutes until the vegetables are heated through and the prawns have turned completely pink. Serve immediately.

Spicy Prawn Stew

per serving;
Calories 199, Fat 3.1g, Sugar 11g, Salt 1.3g
Prep time: 5 minutes
Cook time: 20-25 minutes

- **150g king prawns, raw, peeled and deveined**
- **1 medium courgette, sliced and cut into quarters**
- **1 x 200g can of chopped tomatoes**
- **150ml vegetable stock**
- **1 small onion, peeled and diced**
- **¼ tsp chilli flakes**
- **1 small garlic clove, peeled and finely diced**
- **juice of one lime**
- **black pepper**
- **rapeseed oil spray**

1. Heat a medium saucepan over a low-medium heat. Add a couple of sprays of the rapeseed oil, the onion, garlic, courgette and chilli and cook for 5-6 mins or until softened.

2. Increase the heat to medium-high, add the tomatoes and stock, and cook for 10 minutes.

3. Add the prawns and lime juice. Cook for 5 mins until the prawns turn pink and are just cooked.

4. Season with a little black pepper and serve in a warmed bowl.

TIP
This is great served with chunks of fresh crusty bread!

Baked Salmon
with Courgette and Carrots

per serving:
Calories 348, Fat 21g, Sugar 11g, Salt 0.2g
Prep time: 10 minutes
Cook time: 20 minutes

- **130g salmon fillet**
- **1 large carrot**
- **1 large courgette**
- **1 lemon, cut in half**
- **1 tbsp fresh parsley**
- **fresh ground black**

TIP
Great with potatoes or rice.

1. Pre-heat the oven to 190°C, 375°F, Gas Mark 5.

2. Place a large piece of baking parchment on a baking tray.

3. Using a vegetable peeler, peel strips of carrot and courgette and lay them in a pile on the baking parchment.

4. Place the salmon fillet on top (skin side down) , season with some black pepper. Take one half of the lemon and cut a couple of slices and lay on top of the salmon. Take the juice from the other half and squeeze over the top.

5. Take another piece of baking parchment and lay over the top. Roll up the edges to make a sealed bag.

6. Place in the oven and cook for 20 minutes.

7. Remove from the oven and leave to rest for 2-3 minutes. Carefully open the parchment bag.

8. Sprinkle over the parsley and serve straight away.

Super Quick Mackerel Pate

per serving:
Calories 174, Fat 13g, Sugar 1.5g, Salt 1.1g
Prep time: 5 minutes

- **50g smoked mackerel fillet, skin removed**
- **25g lightest cream cheese**
- **juice of 1 lime**
- **freshly ground black pepper**

1. Place all of the ingredients into a small bowl. Using a fork, mash all of the ingredients together until evenly combined.

2. Serve straight away or store in the fridge for up to 24 hours.

Jacket Fish Pie

per serving:
Calories 353, Fat 9.6g, Sugar 5.4g, Salt 1g
Prep time: 10 minutes
Cook time: 20 minutes

- **1 medium cooked and cooled jacket potato (approx. 160-180g raw weight)**
- **90g mixed chunky boneless fish**
- **25g reduced-fat cheddar cheese**
- **2 tbsps semi-skimmed milk**
- **1 tbsp reduced-fat cream cheese**
- **½ tsp dried dill**
- **freshly ground black pepper**
- **rapeseed oil spray**

1. Preheat the oven to 200°C, Gas mark 6, or use the baking oven in an Aga or similar.

2. Heat a small frying pan, add a couple of sprays of the rapeseed oil and add the mixed diced fish and 1 tbsp of the milk. Reduce the heat slightly and gently poach for 1-2 minutes. Add the dill, and, black pepper and cream cheese, stirring gently to combine. Cook for a further minute then turn off the heat and set aside.

3. Take the top of the cooked baked potato, and gently scoop out the flesh, ensuring you don't break the skin. Place the flesh into a bowl. Place the potato shell in a small shallow ovenproof dish.

4. Add the remaining milk and cheese to the potato flesh and mash together until smooth.

5. Place the fish mixture carefully into the potato shell and top with the mashed potato mixture. Place in the oven and cook for 20-25 minutes until the top is starting to turn a golden colour.

6. To serve, remove the potato from the oven and place on a warmed plate. Serve with a salad or a selection of green vegetables.

Salmon Mousse

per serving;
Calories 252, Fat 9.9g, Sugar 1.5g, Salt 1.1g
Prep time: 5 minutes

- **60g smoked salmon**
- **1 tbsp Philadelphia extra light soft cheese**
- **1 slice medium seeded bread**
- **cracked black pepper**
- **½ tsp lime juice**

1. Place the salmon, cream cheese, cracked black pepper and lime juice into a food processor and blend until smooth.

2. Using a 4.5cm pastry cutter, cut 5 circles from the slice of bread. Place the salmon mousse into a piping bag and pipe a large swirl onto each of the discs.

3. Decorate with some chives (optional). Serve with a green salad or on their own as canapes.

Fish Tacos

per serving;
Calories 449, Fat 7.7g, Sugar 9g, Salt 3g
Prep time: 10 minutes
Cook time: 10 minutes

- **150g cod fillet**
- **3 mini soft tortilla wraps**
- **2 limes**
- **½ tsp smoked paprika**
- **¼ tsp chilli powder**
- **¼ tsp garlic powder**
- **pinch sea salt**
- **1 tbsp low fat mayonnaise**
- **fresh coriander leaves**
- **60g shredded red cabbage**
- **1 medium carrot, cut into matchstick size pieces**

1. Remove the skin from the fish and cut into 9 chunks.

2. Place the sea salt, garlic powder, chilli powder and smoked paprika into a bowl and mix together.

3. Preheat the oven to 190°C, 375°F, Gas Mark 5.

4. Line a baking tray with baking parchment.

5. Place the fish chunks into the spice mix and stir until evenly coated, then place the fish onto the baking tray and bake in the oven for 10 minutes or until the fish is opaque.

6. Mix the mayonnaise with the juice from one of the limes and set aside.

7. Remove the fish from the oven and place 3 fish chunks in the centre of each tortilla.

8. Top with the shredded cabbage and carrot, drizzle with the lime mayonnaise and top with a few coriander leaves.

9. Serve straight away with the remaining lime cut into wedges.

King Scallops

with Thyme Roasted Baby Potatoes

per serving:
Calories 355, Fat 4.1g, Sugar 1.9g, Salt 1g
Prep time: 5 minutes
Cook time: 25-30 minutes

- **4 king scallops**
- **150g baby potatoes cut in half**
- **2 fresh sprigs of thyme**
- **rapeseed oil spray**
- **sea salt and black pepper**
- **few micro herbs for serving (optional)**

1. Preheat the oven to 200°C, 400°F, Gas Mark 6

2. Line a baking tray with baking parchment. Place the cut potatoes onto the tray and spray with a little of the rapeseed oil, and season with a little sea salt. Remove the thyme leaves from the sprigs and sprinkle over the potatoes. Place towards the top of the oven and cook for 20-25 minutes until cooked through.

3. Season the scallops with the salt and pepper.

4. Just a few minutes before the potatoes are cooked, heat a small non-stick frying pan. Add two sprays of the rapeseed oil to the pan then add the scallops, pressing each one down gently to ensure they sear. Cook for 1-2 minutes on each side or until they are golden brown and slightly caramelised.

5. Remove the roasted potatoes from the oven and transfer to a warm plate, top with the scallops and the micro herbs (if using). Serve straight away.

TIP

Thread the scallops onto skewers to make them easier to turn during cooking.

Spicy Prawn Topper

per serving;
Calories 66, Fat 1.3g, Sugar 2.2g, Salt 1g
Prep time: 5 minutes

- **50g cooked peeled prawns**
- **30g lightest cream cheese**
- **pinch of chilli flakes**
- **juice of 1 lime**
- **freshly ground black pepper**

1. In a bowl, mix together the cream cheese, prawns, chilli flakes and lime juice and season to taste with black pepper.

2. Serve as a sandwich/wrap filling or on top of a jacket potato.

King Prawn and Asparagus Linguine

per serving:
Calories 345, Fat 4.1g, Sugar 3.9g, Salt 2.1g
Prep time: 10 minutes
Cook time: 20-25 minutes

- **55g (dry weight) linguine pasta**
- **1 small garlic clove, peeled and finely chopped**
- **150g raw, peeled (tails left on and deveined) king prawns**
- **80g asparagus spears, tirmmed to 5 cm in length**
- **1 vegetable stock cube**
- **3 cherry tomatoes, halved**
- **juice and zest of 1 unwaxed lemon**
- **rapeseed oil**
- **1 spring onion, root removed and finely sliced**
- **1 sprig of fresh oregano or a few fresh basil leaves, chopped**

1. Heat a large pan of water and bring to the boil, add the vegetable stock cube and the linguine and cook until the linguine is cooked to your liking.

2. Heat a frying pan and add a couple of sprays of the rapeseed oil, sliced spring onions, asparagus and the garlic. Stir and cook for 1-2 minutes.

3. Add the prawns and cook until pink on both sides and beginning to curl.

4. Add the cherry tomatoes and cook for a further minute before removing from the heat.

5. Drain the cooked linguine and place back into the pan.

6. Add the prawn and asparagus mixture with the lemon juice and zest to the pasta. Stir gently to evenly combine.

7. Serve straight away.

Salmon, Pepper, Tomato and Honey Kebabs

per serving:
Calories 343, Fat 21g, Sugar 11g, Salt 0.15g
Prep time: 10 minutes
Cook time: 15 minutes

- **135g salmon fillet steak, skin removed**
- **1 small red pepper, deseeded and cut into 6 pieces**
- **1 tomato, cut into quarters**
- **1 tsp honey**
- **Freshly ground black pepper**

You will need two skewers for this recipe.

1. Preheat a grill to high.

2. Cut the salmon fillet into 6 chunks. Thread one piece of pepper onto a skewer followed by a salmon chunk, pepper, tomato quarter, salmon, pepper, tomato quarter and salmon chunk.

3. Repeat the same process for the remaining ingredients on the other skewer.

4. Brush each kebab lightly with the honey – if the honey is difficult to work with, add a couple of drops of hot water to thin it down slightly.

5. Place the kebabs on a grill pan and place under the grill. Carefully turn the kebabs every 3-4 minutes until cooked on all sides.

6. Serve hot or cold with some freshly ground black pepper on top.

TIP

 If you are using wooden skewers, it is a good idea to pre-soak them in water for 20 minutes before using to stop them burning under the grill. This recipe is great for the barbecue!

Leftover Cullen Skink

per serving:
Calories 337, Fat 8.1g, Sugar 14g, Salt 1.3g
Prep time: 10 minutes
Cook time: 15 minutes

- **100g leftover mashed potato**
- **50g leftover cooked cabbage, chopped**
- **200ml whole milk**
- **100g smoked haddock (undyed)**
- **1 small white onion, peeled and diced**
- **1 tbsp freshly chopped parsley**
- **½ tsp dried chives**
- **1 bay leaf**
- **3 black peppercorns**

1. Place the milk into a small saucepan with the dried chives, black peppercorns, and bay leaf. Add the fish and slowly bring to the boil, then reduce to a simmer and cook for 3 minutes.

2. Using a slotted spoon carefully lift out the fish and set aside onto a small plate.

3. Strain the hot milk mixture into a jug and discard the herbs and peppercorns and keep the poaching milk.

4. Add a couple of sprays of the rapeseed oil to the saucepan, add the onion and cook for 2-3 minutes. Add the cooked cabbage and cook for a further minute.

5. Pour the poaching milk into the saucepan with the onions and cabbage, then mix in the mashed potato to get a thicker consistency. Bring to a simmer.

6. Flake the fish on the plate, discarding any skin. Add most of the flaked fish to the saucepan, reserving a little for serving, and stir gently to combine. Cook for a further minute until heated through.

7. Stir in the parsley, and pour into a warmed soup bowl. Top with the remaining flaked fish.

TIP
This recipe uses leftover vegetables, which makes it such a quick meal to make.

Meat

Simple Chicken and Tomato Pasta

per serving:
Calories 452, Fat 3g, Sugar 5.2g, Salt 1.3g
Prep time: 5 minutes
Cook time: 20 minutes

- **1 x 150g chicken breast, skin removed**
- **80g (dry weight) penne pasta**
- **1 tomato, deseeded and diced**
- **1 tbsp tomato puree**
- **salt and pepper to season**
- **a little fresh parsley to serve (optional)**

1. Bring a large pan of water and a pinch of salt to the boil. Add the penne pasta.

2. Cut the chicken into 1cm size cubes.

3. Heat a frying pan until hot, add a couple of sprays of the oil and add the chicken chunks and cook for 5-10 minutes until golden brown.

4. Add the chopped tomato, tomato puree, and 3 tablespoons of the pasta water to make a thin sauce. Stir until evenly coated and season with the salt and pepper.

5. Drain the pasta and add to the chicken mixture. Stir to cover in the light sauce and serve with a little fresh parsley.

TIP
This can be eaten cold and is a great packed lunch option.

Sweet and Sour Chicken
with Rice

per serving:
Calories 466, Fat 2.6g, Sugar 33g, Salt 1.5g
Prep time: 5 minutes
Cook time: 20 minutes

- **1 x 120g small chicken breast, skin removed and cut into chunks**
- **55g (dry weight) basmati rice**
- **1 x 200g can of pineapple chunks in juice**
- **1 small onion, peeled and diced**
- **1 tbsp balsamic vinegar**
- **1 tsp soy sauce**
- **1 tsp dark brown sugar**
- **1 tsp tomato ketchup**
- **1.5 tsp cornflour or 00 grade plain flour**
- **rapeseed oil spray**

1. Bring a saucepan of water to the boil and add the basmati rice.

2. Heat a frying pan until hot and add a couple of sprays of the oil and add the onion and chicken. Cook for 5 minutes.

3. In a jug add the balsamic vinegar, soy sauce, sugar, ketchup, the juice from the canned pineapple and cornflour and whisk until smooth.

4. Add the pineapple chunks to the chicken and stir. Pour in the sweet and sour sauce and gently bring to the boil, stirring all the time. Reduce the heat to a simmer and cook for a further 1-2 minutes.

5. Drain the rice and place on a warmed serving dish. Pour over the sweet and sour chicken and serve straightaway.

Rich Chicken Chasseur

per serving:
Calories 264, Fat 3.3g, Sugar 4.5g, Salt 2.4g
Prep time: 10 minutes
Cook time: 25 minutes

- **1 x 150g skinless and boneless chicken breast**
- **170ml beef stock**
- **60g baby button mushrooms, cleaned and cut in half**
- **2 baby shallots, peeled and chopped**
- **30ml brandy**
- **½ tsp dried tarragon**
- **½ tsp garlic paste, or 1 small garlic clove, peeled and finely diced**
- **rapeseed oil spray**
- **salt and freshly ground black pepper**
- **1 sprig of fresh oregano or a few fresh basil leaves, chopped**

1. Heat a small frying pan over a medium heat. Add a couple of sprays of rapeseed oil then add the garlic paste, chopped shallots and mushrooms. Fry for 2-3 minutes then add the chicken breast and cook on each side until starting to brown.

2. Add the brandy to the pan and stir so that all of the contents are coated and then stir in the tomato puree and dried tarragon. Add the beef stock and stir to combine all of the flavours.

3. Reduce the heat to a simmer, and allow to cook for a further 15-20 minutes. If the sauce gets too thick, thin down with a little water.

4. Season with a little salt and black pepper.

TIP
This is great served with rice or mashed potato.

Sausage Shakshuka

per serving:
Calories 550, Fat 20g, Sugar 22g, Salt 3.2g
Prep time: 5 minutes
Cook time: 25-30 minutes

- **3 chicken chipolata sausages, each cut into 3 pieces**
- **1 x 200g tin of chopped tomatoes**
- **2 small eggs**
- **3 spring onions, cleaned and sliced**
- **1 small red onion, peeled and sliced**
- **1 small red pepper, deseeded and diced**
- **1 small orange pepper, deseeded and diced**
- **1 small clove of garlic, peeled and finely diced**
- **½ tsp smoked paprika**
- **½ tsp cumin seeds**
- **pinch cayenne pepper powder**
- **1 tsp tomato puree**
- **50ml vegetable stock**
- **1 tbsp of fresh coriander leaves**
- **salt and fresh ground black pepper**
- **rapeseed oil spray**

1. Heat a frying pan and spray with a little rapeseed oil. Add the spring onions, red onion, peppers and sausages. Cook until the sausages are starting to take on a little bit of colour and the peppers and onions have started to soften.

2. Add the garlic and cook for a further 2 minutes, then add the cumin seeds and the paprika and cayenne into the frying pan. Stir in the tomato puree and cook for 3-4 minutes. Add the chopped tomatoes and the vegetable stock.

3. Reduce the heat to a simmer and cook for a further 5-10 minutes until the sauce has thickened but is not dry, then stir in the chopped coriander and season with the salt and black pepper.

4. Make two small wells in the tomato mixture and crack an egg into each well. If you have a lid for the frying pan then place it on top: if not then take a large piece of foil and place it shiny side down gently on the top of the frying pan, taking care not to touch the eggs. Cook for 3-4 minutes. Remove the lid or foil and serve straight away. Garnish with fresh coriander leaves.

Quick Chicken Dhansak Curry

per serving:
Calories 321, Fat 5.7g, Sugar 6.3g, Salt 1.4g
Prep time: 5 minutes
Cook time: 20-25 minutes

- **1 x 150g chicken breast – cut in into 9 pieces**
- **½ 400g can of lentil soup**
- **1 small onion, finely diced**
- **1 x 200g tin of chopped tomatoes**
- **1 small clove of garlic, peeled and finely diced**
- **1 ½ tsp garam masala or curry powder**
- **½ tsp turmeric**
- **½ tsp cumin seeds**
- **1 small red chilli, deseeded and finely diced or ⅓ tsp of dried chilli flakes**
- **few fresh coriander leaves to serve**
- **rapeseed oil spray**
- **black pepper**

1. Heat a heavy based large saucepan and add a couple of sprays of the rapeseed oil. Add the onion, garlic and chilli and cook gently until softened – about 2-3 minutes.

2. Add the garam masala, turmeric, cumin seeds and chicken pieces. Stir and cook for a further 3-4 minutes until the chicken starts to brown.

3. Add the tomatoes and lentil soup. Bring to the boil then reduce the heat and simmer (stirring occasionally), cook for a further 10-15 minutes until the sauce has thickened.

4. Serve in a warmed bowl topped with freshly ground black pepper and the fresh coriander leaves.

Lamb Kofta

per serving:
Calories 210, Fat 14g, Sugar 0g, Salt 1.2g
Prep time: 5 minutes
Cook time: 10 minutes

- **140g lean lamb mince**
- **1 tsp ground cumin**
- **1 tbsp fresh coriander leaves, finely chopped**
- **1 clove of garlic, peeled and finely chopped**
- **pinch of salt**
- **pinch of black pepper**

1. Place all of the ingredients into a non-metallic bowl and mix together so everything is evenly combined.

2. Divide into 3 portions to create 3 sausage shaped, koftas.

3. Heat a frying pan to hot and add the koftas. Cook for 4-5 minutes on each side.

4. Serve hot or cold. These are great served with a light herby salad and flatbreads.

Spicy Turkey Burgers

per serving:
Calories 470, Fat 4.8g, Sugar 7.8g, Salt 1.4g
Prep time: (includes chilling) 70 minutes
Cook time: 10 minutes

- **150g turkey mince**
- **3 mini brioche rolls**
- **1 small onion, finely chopped**
- **25ml semi skimmed milk**
- **½ slice of wholegrain bread**
- **1 tbsp fresh coriander leaves**
- **1 small red chilli, top removed**
- **1 tsp of pork seasoning or mixed herbs**
- **freshly ground black pepper**

TIP
Make these the day before and leave in the fridge until you're ready to cook.

1. Heat a small frying pan, add a couple of sprays of the rapeseed oil then add the onion and cook gently until softened. Remove from the heat and allow to cool.

2. Roughly tear the bread into pieces and place in a bowl, pour over the milk and allow to sit for 3-5 minutes until all the milk is absorbed.

3. In a food processor add everything except the mince, and blitz for 1 minute. Now add in the mince and blitz again for another minute until evenly mixed. The mixture will look a little loose, but don't worry.

4. Cover in cling film and chill for an hour or so. This will allow the flavours to develop.

5. Re-heat the frying pan.

6. Divide the mixture into 3 balls and flatten into 3 small burgers (it will be a bit sticky) and add to the pan. Cook for 2-3 minutes on each side turning only once.

7. Serve in warmed mini brioche roll topped with some fresh herbs (optional) or just on top of a salad.

Simple Chicken Korma

per serving:
Calories 305, Fat 5g, Sugar 15g, Salt 1g
Prep time: 5 minutes
Cook time: 20 minutes

- **1 x 130g diced chicken breast**
- **200ml of coconut milk**
- **1 small onion, peeled and finely diced**
- **1½ tsp plain flour (00 grade is best)**
- **1 tsp garam masala or curry powder**
- **½ tsp turmeric**
- **1cm cube of fresh ginger peeled and finely chopped or grated**
- **1 small clove of garlic, peeled and finely chopped**
- **1 tbsp fresh coriander, roughly chopped**
- **50ml of whole milk**
- **rapeseed oil spray**

1. Add the flour and the chicken cubes to a medium sized bowl and stir until the chicken is evenly coated in the flour.

2. Heat a non-stick saucepan and add a couple of sprays of the rapeseed oil, onion and garlic and cook until soft.

3. Add the garam masala, ginger and turmeric to the onion and garlic mixture, stir and cook for 1 minute.

4. Add the chicken and excess flour to the saucepan and stir to evenly coat with the spice mixture. Continue cooking until the chicken has been sealed and is starting to take on the colour of the spices.

5. Gently add the coconut milk and the milk. Slowly bring to the boil, stirring all the time to ensure the sauce does not split, reduce to a simmer and cook for a further 10–15 minutes until the sauce has thickened and the chicken is cooked.

6. Just before serving stir in the fresh coriander and serve.

7. Delicious with rice or naan bread or even poured over a jacket potato.

Duck a L'Orange

per serving:
Calories 331, Fat 16g, Sugar 21g, Salt 1.1g
Prep time: 5 minutes
Cook time: (including resting time) 25 minutes

1. Preheat the oven to 200°C, 400°F, Gas Mark 6. Prepare the duck by removing all the skin with a sharp knife. Season with salt and pepper and rub it into the duck.

2. Preheat a non-stick pan until hot. Add the duck and seal for 3-4 minutes until brown then remove and place on a baking tray in a preheated oven to finish cooking for 10-15 minutes.

3. In a small bowl add the juice and zest from one and a half of the oranges, cornflour, marmalade and balsamic vinegar. Whisk until blended.

4. Return the pan to the stove and add the chicken stock and orange juice mixture and cook until a glossy sauce is created. Cut two slices from the remaining half of the orange and add to the sauce. Allow to gently cook for a further minute.

5. Remove the duck from the oven and cover with foil, allowing to rest for 5 minutes. Drain away the meat juices from the duck into the sauce.

6. Serve the duck on a warmed plate with the sauce and cooked orange slices poured over the top. Delicious served with vegetables.

- **1 x 230g duck leg**
- **2 large oranges**
- **2 tsp marmalade**
- **2 tsp balsamic vinegar**
- **1 tsp cornflour**
- **120 ml chicken stock**

Chicken and Bacon BBQ Stir-fry

per serving:
Calories 316, Fat 12g, Sugar 14g, Salt 1.6g
Prep time: 5 minutes
Cook time: 15-20 minutes

- **1 rasher smoked back bacon, excess fat removed**
- **1 x 100g skinless chicken breast, cut into strips**
- **160g of mixed stir-fry fresh vegetables**
- **2 spring onions, cleaned and sliced**
- **1 tbsp BBQ sauce (for a homemade version see page 73)**

1. Preheat a non-stick frying pan and dry-fry the chicken and bacon until just cooked.

2. Add the sliced spring onion and mixed stir-fry vegetables, cook for a further 2-3 minutes.

3. Add the BBQ sauce and stir to combine. Cook for a further minute then serve and eat straightaway.

Terriaki Chicken and Rice

per serving:
Calories 428, Fat 7.9g, Sugar 11g, Salt 1.6g
Prep time: 10 minutes
Cook time: 15 minutes

- **1 x 125g approx weight, chicken thigh, boned, skinned and sliced into strips.**
- **55g (dry weight) basmati rice**
- **1 tbsp dark soy sauce or tamari gluten free soy sauce**
- **2 tsps clear honey**
- **1 tsp sesame oil**
- **¼ tsp sesame seeds**
- **1 spring onion, cleaned, root removed and sliced (optional for garnish only)**

1. Bring a pan of water to the boil.

2. Put the honey, sesame oil and soy sauce in a bowl and mix well. Add the chicken strips into the bowl, stir well to coat and leave to marinate for 5 minutes.

3. Add the rice and boil for 10-12 minutes.

4. Heat a frying pan and add a couple of sprays of rapeseed oil. Carefully remove the chicken slices from the marinade, reserving the marinade, and fry for 2-3 minutes on each side, or until completely cooked through. Remove the chicken from the frying pan and set aside, keeping warm. Add the remaining marinade to the frying pan and bring to the boil for 1 minute, then remove from the heat.

5. Drain the rice and place on to a warmed plate, top with the chicken and thickened sauce, sprinkle over the sesame seeds and sliced spring onion (optional).

Super Quick Sausage Bagel Pizza

per serving:
Calories 423, Fat 8.1g, Sugar 4.8g, Salt 2.9g
Prep time: 5 minutes
Cook time: 10-12 minutes

- **1 wholemeal bagel**
- **1 reduced fat sausage**
- **35g low fat cheese, grated**
- **1 tbsp tomato puree**
- **½ tsp mixed dried herbs**

1. Preheat the oven to 200°C, 400°F, Gas Mark 6.

2. Cut the bagel in half and place onto a non-stick baking tray, cut side up.

3. Place the tomato puree, mixed herbs and 1 tsp water into a bowl and mix until combined.   Divide the tomato mixture in two and spread over the top of the cut sides.

4. Sprinkle the grated cheese over the two bagels.

5. Gently run a sharp knife down the length of the sausage, just to pierce the skin. Pull the skin away and discard.   Crumble the sausage meat equally over the bagels.

6. Place in the oven and cook for 10 -12 minutes until the sausage has started to go golden brown.

7. Eat hot or cold.

Quick Bacon Spaghetti Carbonara

- **60g extra light low fat cream cheese**
- **50g (dry weight) spaghetti**
- **3 rashers lean back bacon**
- **freshly ground black pepper**

per serving:
Calories 348, Fat 4.2g, Sugar 4.3g, Salt 2.7g
Prep time: 5 minutes
Cook time: 15 minutes

1. Cook the spaghetti in boiling water for 10 minutes.

2. While the spaghetti is cooking, dry fry bacon and then cut the bacon into small strips.

3. Drain the spaghetti and add the bacon and cream cheese. Return to a low heat and gently stir until the cheese has melted and has coated the pasta and bacon.

4. Season with freshly ground black pepper. Serve in a warm pasta bowl.

Simple Pork and Noodle Stir-fry

per serving:
Calories 448, Fat 7g, Sugar 12g, Salt 1.6g
Prep time: 5 minutes
Cook time: 15 minutes

- **1 x 100g lean pork loin steak, visible fat removed**
- **1 small courgette, cut into small sticks**
- **1 small carrot, peeled and cut into small sticks**
- **150g fresh/ready to use egg noodles**
- **3 chestnut mushrooms**
- **1 tsp honey**
- **1 tsp soy sauce**
- **½ tsp dried chilli flakes**
- **pinch black sesame seeds (optional)**
- **rapeseed oil spray**

1. Heat a heavy-based frying pan and add a couple of sprays of the rapeseed oil. Add the pork slices and fry for 3-4 minutes, stirring occasionally.

2. Add the courgette, carrot and mushrooms to the pork and cook for a further 3-4 minutes.

3. Add the soy sauce, honey and chilli flakes and stir to coat all the ingredients.

4. Add the noodles and cook for a further 2-3 minutes until the noodles are heated through.

5. Serve in a warmed bowl with the black sesame seeds sprinkled over (if using) and season with a little extra soy sauce if required.

Chorizo and Tomato Pasta

per serving:
Calories 479, Fat 14g, Sugar 6.9g, Salt 2g
Prep time: 5 minutes
Cook time: 15-20 minutes

- **80g (dry weight) penne pasta**
- **45g reduced fat chorizo sausage, sliced**
- **150g tomato passata**
- **½ tsp dried mixed herbs**
- **½ tsp smoked paprika**

1. Heat a saucepan of water until boiling, then add the pasta and cook for 10-15 minutes until cooked but not soggy.

2. Whilst the pasta is cooking dry fry the chorizo slices for 2-3 minutes, then add the tomato passata, smoked paprika and mixed herbs.

3. Drain the pasta, add to the tomato and chorizo sauce and stir to combine.

4. Serve straightaway in a warm pasta bowl.

Bacon and Asparagus Pasta

per serving:
Calories 394, Fat 7.4g, Sugar 2.7g, Salt 2g
Prep time: 5 minutes
Cook time: 20 minutes

- **80g (dry weight) penne pasta**
- **60g asparagus spears, cut in half**
- **2 rashers back bacon, visible fat removed and sliced into strips**
- **4 fresh basil leaves, torn in half**
- **1 vegetable stock pot**
- **½ tsp parmesan, grated for garnish**

1. Cook the pasta in a large pan of boiling water with the vegetable stock pot.

2. Meanwhile, heat a non-stick frying pan, then dry-fry the bacon for 4-5 minutes.

3. Two minutes before the pasta is cooked, add the asparagus spears to the pasta pan, cook for two minutes, then drain the pasta and asparagus.

4. Add the pasta, asparagus and basil leaves to the bacon, stir to combine and then transfer to a warmed plate, grate over a little parmesan cheese and serve immediately.

Pork Loin Chop
with a Balsamic Reduction

per serving:
Calories 527, Fat 35g, Sugar 7.1g, Salt 1.3g
Prep time: 5 minutes
Cook time: 15-20 minutes

- **1 pork chop (approx 220g), fat trimmed**
- **1tbsp balsamic vinegar**
- **½ tsp dark brown muscovado sugar**
- **salt and black pepper**

1. Dry the chop using kitchen paper, then season it with a little salt and black pepper on both sides.

2. Heat a small frying pan until hot, add the pork chop and dry fry on one side for 6-7 minutes. Turn the pork over and cook on the other side for 6-7 minutes, until cooked through.

3. Remove the pork chop from the frying pan and place on a warmed plate to rest and wipe the pan clean of any fat.

4. Add the balsamic vinegar, sugar and 1 tbsp water to the frying pan.

5. Cook, stirring until sugar is dissolved and liquid is thickened slightly. This will take approximately 1-2 minutes.

6. Reduce heat to medium, add the pork with any juices from the plate to the frying pan. Coat the chop in the sauce.

7. Transfer the chop to a warmed plate and drizzle over any remaining juices. Served with vegetables.

Beef Vindaloo and Rice

per serving:
Calories 496, Fat 12g, Sugar 13g, Salt 1.9g
Prep time: 10 minutes
Cook time: 75 minutes

- **120g beef steak, sliced into strips across the grain**
- **1 x 200g can of chopped tomatoes**
- **55g (dry weight) basmati rice**
- **200ml beef stock**
- **1 white onion, peeled and sliced**
- **1½ tbsps vindaloo curry paste**
- **1 clove of fresh garlic, peeled and finely chopped**
- **1½cm fresh ginger root, peeled and finely chopped**
- **1.5 tsps garam masala**
- **¼ tsp turmeric**
- **2 cardamom pods (optional)**

1. Heat a non-stick frying pan and add the onion, ginger, garam masala and garlic. Cook until softened, then remove and keep warm.

2. Add the beef to the frying pan and fry until browned. Return the onion spiced mixture to the frying pan with the curry paste, tomatoes and stock.

3. Bring to the boil, then reduce down to a simmer and cook for an hour or until the beef is tender.

4. Once the beef is cooked, bring a pan of water to the boil. Add the turmeric, cardamom pods, if using, and the rice. Bring to the boil and cook for 10-15 minutes until the rice is tender.

5. Drain the rice and place on a warm plate, top with the beef curry and serve straightaway.

Gnocchi with Tomato and Parma Ham

per serving:
Calories 419, Fat 7.4g, Sugar 8.2g, Salt 3.2g
Prep time: 5 minutes
Cook time: 15 minutes

- **160g fresh gnocchi**
- **3 slices parma ham (approx 40g),
  cut into strips**
- **1 x 200g tin of chopped tomatoes**
- **¼ tsp smoked paprika**
- **10g low fat cheese, grated**

1. Heat a non-stick frying pan on a medium heat and add the ham strips, cook for 2-3 minutes or until browned. Add the chopped tomatoes and paprika and bring to the boil, then reduce the heat to a gentle simmer.

2. Bring a large pan of water to the boil, then gently add the gnocchi stirring once to separate. Cook for 2 minutes or until the gnocchi floats to the top, then drain.

3. Add the cooked gnocchi to the ham and tomato sauce, stirring gently to evenly coat the gnocchi.

4. Transfer to a warm serving dish and top with the grated cheese.

5. Serve straightaway.

Simple Beef Stir-fry

per serving:
Calories 246, Fat 10g, Sugar 8.5g, Salt 1.5g
Prep time: 15 minutes
Cook time: 15 minutes

- **100g rump steak cut into strips**
- **160g fresh vegetable stir-fry mix**
- **2 spring onions, cleaned and sliced**
- **1 tsp soy sauce**
- **2 tsp sweet chilli sauce**
- **juice and zest of 1 lime**
- **rapeseed oil spray**

1. Place the beef in a bowl with the soy sauce, spring onions, sweet chilli sauce and lime, stir to combine, coating the beef in the sauce and leave to marinate for 10 minutes.

2. Preheat a frying pan, add a spray of rapeseed oil and stir fry the beef and marinade for 3-4 minutes.

3. Add vegetables and cook for a further 3-4 minutes.

4. Serve straightaway on a warmed plate.

Spaghetti Bolognese

per serving:
Calories 481, Fat 11g, Sugar 13g, Salt 1.4g
Prep time: 5 minutes
Cook time: 35 minutes

- **60g fresh beef mince**
- **50g fresh pork mince**
- **50g (dry weight) spaghetti**
- **1 x 200g tin of chopped tomatoes**
- **1 small onion, finely diced**
- **1 cloves of garlic, peeled and finely chopped**
- **60ml red wine**
- **2 tsp tomato puree**
- **½ beef or vegetable stock cube**
- **1 tsp dried italian mixed herbs**
- **black pepper to taste**
- **fresh basil leaves to serve (optional)**
- **rapeseed oil spray**

1. Heat a saucepan and then add a spray of the oil and add the onions and garlic, cook gently until softened.

2. Turn up the heat slightly and add the beef and pork mince a bit at a time (this will help to stop the temperature of the pan cooling and stop the mince from boiling rather than frying) and cook until the meat has browned.

3. Add the tomatoes, tomato puree, wine, herbs and stock cube to the mince and stir until all the ingredients have combined.

4. Reduce the heat and allow to simmer until the tomatoes have softened and the sauce has reduced – this will take about 25 minutes.

5. 15 minutes before the Bolognese has finished cooking, heat up some water in a separate pan and cook the spaghetti.

6. Season the Bolognese sauce with a little black pepper if required.

7. Drain the pasta, and serve on a warm plate or in a pasta bowl, and top with the Bolognese sauce and basil leaves (if using).

Korean Beef with Noodles

per serving:
Calories 431, Fat 7g, Sugar 8.9g, Salt 2.1g
Prep time: 10 minutes
Cook time: 10 minutes

- **100g rump steak cut into strips**
- **150g fresh/ready to use egg noodles**
- **1 small green pepper, deseeded and sliced**
- **1 spring onion, cleaned and thinly sliced**
- **1 tsp grated fresh ginger**
- **2 tsp soy sauce**
- **1 small garlic clove, peeled and diced**
- **½ tsp brown sugar**
- **juice and zest of 1 lime**
- **rapeseed oil spray**

1. Place the beef in a bowl with the ginger, sugar, soy sauce, spring onion and lime, stir to combine coating the beef in the sauce and leave to marinate for 10 minutes.

2. Preheat a frying pan, add a spray of rapeseed oil and stir fry the pepper and garlic for 3-4 minutes.

3. Add the beef and marinade sauce to the pan and cook for a further 2-3 minutes.

4. Add the noodles, stir and cook for another 2-3 minutes until heated through.

5. Serve straightaway on a warmed plate.

Rich Oxtail Stew

per serving:
Calories 508, Fat 26g, Sugar 10g, Salt 2.1g
Prep time: 5 minutes
Cook time: 2 hours

- **250g oxtail, excess fat removed**
- **1 large stick of celery, cut into 1cm chunks**
- **1 carrot, peeled and cut into 1cm chunks**
- **120ml pale ale**
- **230ml beef stock**
- **1 bay leaf**
- **black pepper**

1. Heat a heavy based small frying pan or saucepan that has a lid until hot. Add the oxtail and fry until sealed and brown on all sides.

2. Add the celery and carrot and cook for a further 2-3 minutes.

3. Pour in the ale and stock, add the bay leaf and a little black pepper and bring to the boil. Reduce the heat to a gentle simmer and place the lid on the pan.

4. Leave to cook slowly for 1-2 hours or until the meat starts to fall away from the bone.

5. Using a slotted spoon carefully lift out the oxtail and transfer to a warmed serving dish.

6. Bring the remaining liquid and veg back to the boil for 2-3 minutes to thicken the sauce. Remove the bay leaf and discard. Pour over the top of the oxtail and serve straightaway with a selection of vegetables.

Rich Beef Casserole

per serving:
Calories 389, Fat 16g, Sugar 12g, Salt 1.5g
Prep time: 30 minutes
Cook time: 70 minutes

- **120g chuck steak, cut into 2cm cubes**
- **80ml red wine**
- **1 bouquet garni**
- **pinch black pepper**
- **1tsp tomato puree**
- **1 small garlic clove, crushed**
- **1 carrot**
- **1 small onion, peeled and diced**
- **200ml beef stock**
- **1½ tsp plain flour**

1. Place the meat, red wine, bouquet garni, black pepper and garlic into a non-metallic bowl. Cover with cling film and leave to marinate for 30 minutes.

2. Remove the crushed garlic clove and the bouquet garni from the marinade and discard. Drain the beef from the marinade ensuring you keep the marinade in a jug to use later.

3. Toss the beef cubes in the plain flour until evenly coated.

4. Preheat the oven to 160°C, 320°F, Gas Mark 3.

5. Heat a non-stick saucepan and gently fry the beef and cook until brown on the outside. Now add the onion, carrot and cook for a further 2 minutes.

6. Slowly add the beef stock, tomato puree and the marinade liquor, stir and bring to the boil. Turn the heat off and transfer carefully to a small ovenproof casserole dish. Cook for 1 hour until the meat is tender.

7. Serve hot with vegetables.

Lamb Shank

per serving:
Calories 504, Fat 11g, Sugar 4.3g, Salt 0.7g
Prep time: 15 minutes
Cook time: 1-2 hours

- **1 x 350g lamb shank, trimmed**
- **1 bay leaf**
- **150ml good quality medium dry white wine**
- **1 sprigs of fresh rosemary**
- **2 garlic cloves peeled and cut in half**
- **salt and freshly milled black pepper**

1. Preheat the oven to 180°C, 360°F, Gas Mark 4.

2. Using a small knife make 4 splits around the sides of the shank and a single slit at the top where the bone and flesh meet. Place half a garlic clove in each of the slits around the sides and a sprig of rosemary in the top slit. Season with the salt and black pepper.

3. Place the shanks in a small heavy based deep casserole dish. Stand the shank up in the casserole dish so the bone shaft sticks out the top. Add the bay leaf and the white wine to the casserole dish. Cover with foil (shiny side down) and place in the oven and cook for 1-2 hours or until the meat is tender.

4. Remove from the oven and allow to rest for 5 minutes before serving. Serve with a selection of vegetables.

Sticky Chicken Kebabs

per serving:
Calories 276, Fat 6.7g, Sugar 17g, Salt 2.3g
Prep time: (including chilling) 65 minutes
Cook time: 20 minutes

- **1 x 150g skinless medium chicken breast**
- **1 tbsp honey**
- **1 tbsp soy sauce**
- **1 tsp sesame oil**
- **1 tsp fresh ginger, finely grated**

TIP
Use the remaining marinade to baste the chicken during cooking.
These can also be cooked on a barbecue.

1. Cut the chicken breast into 6 long strips

2. In a bowl mix together the honey, soy sauce, sesame oil and fresh ginger.

3. Add the chicken strips to the marinade and stir until the chicken is evenly coated. Cover the bowl with cling film and chill in the fridge for an hour or overnight.

4. When ready to cook, preheat the oven to 190°C, 375°F, Gas Mark 5. Line a large baking tray with baking parchment or foil

5. Thread the chicken strips equally between 6 mini skewers, and lay them on the baking tray. Place in the oven and cook for 20 minutes, turning over after the first 10 minutes.

6. Serve with salad, couscous or rice.

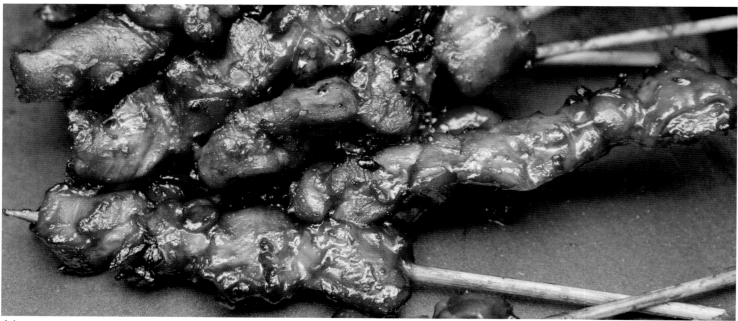

Red Onion Stuffed with Lamb

per serving:
Calories 329, Fat 12g, Sugar 21g, Salt 1.2g
Prep time: 5 minutes
Cook time: 45 minutes

- **120g lean lamb mince**
- **3 medium red onions**
- **½ small red pepper, deseeded and finely diced**
- **½ tsp dried oregano**
- **½ tsp dried basil**
- **1 tbsp fresh mint leaves, finely chopped**
- **1 clove of garlic, peeled and finely chopped**
- **pinch of salt**
- **pinch of black pepper**
- **rapeseed oil spray**

1. Preheat the oven to 190°C, 375°F, Gas Mark 5.

2. Top and tail the onions and remove the outer layer of skin. Gently push out the centre part of the onion (and reserve to use later in the recipe) so that you have about five-eighths thickness of the onion shell.

3. Finely dice the centre part of the onion and place in a bowl, adding the mince and remaining ingredients. Mix together well and divide into three. Stuff each onion with one portion of the mixture and place in a non-metallic dish.

4. Spray each onion with a little of the rapeseed oil and bake in the oven for 40-45 minutes until the onion shell is tender.

5. Serve hot with mixed vegetables.

Chilli Con Carne
with Rice

per serving:
Calories 541, Fat 8.8g, Sugar 16g, Salt 0.9g
Prep time: 5 minutes
Cook time: 20-25 minutes

- **120g lean minced beef**
- **1 x 200g can chopped tomatoes**
- **½ 210g can red kidney beans, drained and rinsed**
- **55g (dry weight) basmati rice**
- **1 small onion, peeled and sliced**
- **1 small red pepper, deseeded and sliced**
- **1 small clove of garlic, peeled and diced**
- **2 tsp tomato puree**
- **½ tsp chilli powder**
- **½ tsp cocoa powder (optional)**
- **rapeseed oil spray**

1. Heat a saucepan and add a couple of sprays of the rapeseed oil, fry the garlic, pepper and onion for 2-3 minutes.

2. Add the mince beef and cook until browned (add a little at a time so the pan does not lose temperature and the meat caramelises properly).

3. Add the tomatoes, tomato puree, kidney beans, cocoa powder if using and chilli powder. Stir and cook over a low heat for 15-20 minutes or until the sauce is thicker.

4. In the meantime, bring a pan of water to the boil and cook the rice.

5. Drain the rice and place in a warm bowl, top with the chilli and serve straightaway.

TIP
Swap the cocoa powder for a 2cm square piece of dark chocolate – adding dark chocolate makes the chilli richer in flavour.

One Pot Beef and Chunky Veg Casserole

per serving:
Calories 497, Fat 21g, Sugar 13g, Salt 1.7g
Prep time: 10 minutes
Cook time: 2-2.5 hours

- **150g chuck steak or shin of beef, cut into chunks**
- **150g new baby potatoes, quartered**
- **1 small onion, peeled and chopped**
- **1 large carrot, peeled and cut into chunks**
- **300ml beef stock**
- **2 tsp tomato puree**
- **1 tsp of Worcestershire sauce**
- **½ tsp paprika**
- **2 tsp plain flour**
- **1 bay leaf**
- **black pepper**
- **rapeseed oil spray**

1. Preheat the oven to 165°C, 325°F, Gas Mark 3.

2. Heat a heavy based pan suitable for the oven (if you don't have one, you can transfer the ingredients to a casserole dish just before going into the oven), add a couple of sprays of the rapeseed oil, chopped onion, carrot, and potatoes. Gently fry for 2-3 minutes until they start to colour.

3. Add the plain flour and stir until everything is evenly coated. Add the beef stock, tomato puree, paprika, Worcestershire sauce and bay leaf. Stir to combine then add the beef chunks. Bring to a simmer and then cover and put in the oven. (At this point you could transfer to a casserole dish with a lid or a slow cooker.)

4. Cook for 2 hours, or until the meat is tender.

5. Remove bay leaf and season with a little black pepper. Serve hot.

Sausage Meatballs and Spaghetti

per serving:
Calories 513, Fat 6.4g, Sugar 8.8g, Salt 3.7g
Prep time: 5 minutes
Cook time: 20 minutes

- **50g (dry weight) spaghetti**
- **3 x 95% fat free pork sausages**
- **150g tomato passata**
- **1 tbsp tomato puree**
- **½ tsp dried basil**
- **½ tsp dried oregano**
- **black pepper**
- **a little parmesan cheese to garnish (optional)**

1. Using a sharp knife, carefully put a slit down the side of each sausage and remove the skin and discard.

2. Shape each sausage into a ball shape.

3. Preheat a frying pan and add the sausage meatballs, browning on all sides. Reduce the heat and add the passata, puree and dried herbs. Stir gently to combine and keep the heat to a low simmer.

4. Bring a large pan of water to the boil and add the spaghetti and cook for 10-12 minutes.

5. Drain the spaghetti and place in the middle of a warmed plate. Season the meatball sauce with a little black pepper and top the spaghetti with the meatballs and sauce.

6. Garnish with a little parmesan cheese (optional).

Vegetables

Sweet Potato and Chickpea Curry

per serving:
Calories 416, Fat 3.8g, Sugar 12g, Salt 0.85g
Prep time: 5 minutes
Cook time: 25 minutes

- **40g canned chickpeas, drained**
- **140g sweet potatoes, peeled and diced into 1cm cubes**
- **55g (dry weight) basmati rice**
- **½ small red pepper, deseeded and diced**
- **a little fresh coriander, to serve (optional)**
- **1 spring onion, cleaned, root removed and chopped**
- **1cm piece of fresh ginger root, grated**
- **½ tsp dry chilli flakes**
- **1 tsp garam masala**
- **1 tsp turmeric**
- **½ tsp fennel seeds**
- **½ tsp mixed spice**
- **120ml vegetable stock**
- **1 small garlic clove, peeled and finely**

1. Heat a non-stick frying pan over medium heat, add a couple of sprays of rapeseed oil and fry the chopped spring onion, red pepper, diced sweet potato and garlic for 3-5 minutes. Stir in ginger, garam masala, fennel seeds, mixed spice, chilli and turmeric.

2. Add the stock and chickpeas to the frying pan, bring to the boil, then reduce to a simmer and cook for 15-20 minutes until the liquid has absorbed and the sweet potato is tender.

3. In the meantime bring a pan of water to the boil. Add the rice and cook. Drain and keep warm.

4. To serve place the rice on a warmed plate, top with the curry and sprinkle over the fresh coriander if using.

Roasted Cauliflower and Avocado Tacos

per serving:
Calories 505, Fat 23g, Sugar 9.7g, Salt 1.2g
Prep time: 10 minutes
Cook time: 20 minutes

- **3 mini soft tortillas**
- **140g raw cauliflower florets**
- **½ tsp chilli powder**
- **a little fresh parsley or fresh coriander, optional**
- **60g raw red cabbage, sliced**
- **1 pickled green chilli, sliced**
- **70g avocado flesh**
- **pinch salt**
- **rapeseed oil spray**
- **5g desiccated coconut**

1. Preheat the oven to 220°C, 425°F Gas Mark 8.

2. Place the cauliflower florets onto a non-stick baking tray. Lightly spray with the rapeseed oil.

3. Place the desiccated coconut, salt and chilli powder into a small bowl and mix together. Sprinkle the powder mix over the cauliflower florets. Place in the oven and bake for 15-20 minutes.

4. Five minutes before the cauliflower has finished cooking, peel, de-stone and slice the avocado. Wrap the tortillas in some foil and place in the oven to warm for 2-3 minutes.

5. Remove the cauliflower and tortillas from the oven. Divide the red cabbage between the four tortillas, repeat with the sliced avocado and then the crunchy cauliflower. Add a couple of slices of pickled chilli to each and sprinkle over some of the fresh herbs and serve straightaway.

Cheese Quesadillas

per serving:
Calories 282, Fat 4.4g, Sugar 1.5g, Salt 1.4g
Prep time: 5 minutes
Cook time: 8 minutes

1.Preheat a small frying pan. Place one tortilla wrap in the pan and top with the grated cheese and a little black pepper, then top with the remaining wrap.

2. Cook for 2-3 minutes on one side then carefully turn over the quesdadilla and cook on the other side for 2 minutes or until the cheese is melted and the wraps have taken on a golden colour.

3. Remove from the frying pan, place on a chopping board and cut into 6. Serve straight away - be careful as the inside will be hot.

- **freshly ground black pepper**
- **35g less than 5% fat cheese, finely grated**
- **2 plain mini tortilla wraps**

Aubergine and Chickpea Tagine

per serving:
Calories 178, Fat 4.5g, Sugar 13g, Salt 2.3g
Prep time: 5 minutes
Cook time: 35 minutes

- **1 small aubergine, diced**
- **1 small red onion**
- **½ x 210g can of chickpeas, drained**
- **1 x 200g can of chopped tomatoes**
- **1 garlic clove, peeled and diced**
- **2 tsps tagine paste**
- **juice and zest of 1 large orange**

1.Heat a nonstick frying pan and dry-fry the onions and garlic until soft and lightly coloured.

2. Add the aubergine and tagine paste and continue to cook to brown the aubergine.

3. Add the tomatoes, orange juice, zest, chickpeas and stock cube. Cover with a lid and simmer gently for 30 minutes.

TIP
Great served with cauliflower rice – see page 76.

Healthy Spinach and Ricotta Cannelloni

per serving:
Calories 413, Fat 15g, Sugar 11g, Salt 1.6g
Prep time: 5 minutes
Cook time: 20 minutes

- **140g baby spinach**
- **3 cannelloni tubes**
- **120g lightest cream cheese**
- **80g ricotta cheese**
- **30ml semi skimmed milk**
- **1 tsp parmesan cheese**
- **pinch chilli powder**
- **salt and black pepper**
- **¼ tsp freshly grated nutmeg**

1. Put the spinach in a large colander and pour over a kettle of boiling water to wilt it. Allow to cool and then squeeze out the excess water.

2. Roughly chop the spinach and mix in a large bowl with ricotta. Season well with the salt, pepper, chilli powder and the nutmeg.

3. Preheat the oven to 190°C, 375°F, Gas Mark 5.

4. Fill each tube with equal amounts of the spinach and cheese mix and place in a small oven proof dish.

5. In a small bowl beat together the light cream cheese with the milk and pour over the cannelloni tubes.

6. Bake in the oven for 20-25 minutes.

7. Remove from the oven and sprinkle with the parmesan cheese and serve straightaway.

Aubergine, Courgette and Tomato Bake

per serving;
Calories 275, Fat 13g, Sugar 8.5g, Salt 2.2g
Prep time: 10 minutes
Cook time: 40 minutes

- **1 medium courgette, top removed and sliced**
- **1 medium aubergine, top removed and cut into 1 cm slices**
- **50g low-fat cheese**
- **salt and freshly ground black pepper**
- **160ml hot vegetable stock**
- **100g mixed coloured cherry tomatoes, halved**

TIP
This will serve 2 people as a side.
This can be eaten cold.

1. Preheat the the oven to 200°C, 400°F Gas Mark 6, or use the top oven in an Aga or similar.

2. Layer the aubergine, courgettes and tomato halves in a small casserole dish. Pour over the hot vegetable stock and season with a little salt and freshly ground black pepper.

3. Place in the oven and cook for 25 minutes. Carefully remove from the oven and sprinkle over the grated cheese. Return to the oven for a further 15 minutes or until the cheese is melted and golden. Remove from the oven and serve with warm crusty bread or as a side dish.

Cherry Tomato Spaghetti

per serving:
Calories 265, Fat 3g, Sugar 8.9g, Salt 0.01g
Prep time: 5 minutes
Cook time: 15 minutes

- **12 cherry tomatoes, cut in half**
- **60g (dry weight) spaghetti**
- **50g tomato passata**
- **rapeseed oil spray**
- **¼ tsp chilli powder**
- **fresh parsley – to garnish, optional**

1. Cook the spaghetti in boiling water for 10 minutes.

2. While the spaghetti is cooking, heat a small frying pan and add a couple of sprays of rapeseed oil. Add the cherry tomatoes, passata and chilli powder. Gently cook until the tomatoes soften.

3. Drain the spaghetti and add the tomato sauce. Stir gently.

4. Pile on to the middle of a warmed pasta bowl and top with a little freshly chopped parsley and black pepper if required.

Courgette, Smoked Paprika & Honey

per serving:
Calories 215, Fat 7.1g, Sugar 26g, Salt 1g
Prep time: 5 minutes
Cook time: 10 minutes

- **150g courgettes, diced**
- **160g fresh vegetable stir fry mix**
- **50g fresh bean sprouts**
- **1 small red pepper, deseeded and diced**
- **80g chestnut mushrooms, sliced**
- **1½ tsps smoked paprika**
- **2 tsps honey**
- **1 tsp soy sauce**
- **2 spring onions, cleaned and thinly sliced**

1. Preheat a non-stick frying pan. Add the courgettes and paprika to the pan and cook over a high heat for 2-3 minutes. Add the onion, pepper and mushrooms and cook for 1 minute more.

2. Add the soy sauce, honey, stir-fry vegetables and beansprouts. Toss well together until heated through and serve.

Stuffed Artichoke

per serving:
Calories 364, Fat 11g, Sugar 9.8g, Salt 2.4g
Prep time: 10 minutes
Cook time: 20 minutes

- **1 whole artichoke (approx. 500g)**
- **50ml dry white wine**
- **30g of breadcrumbs**
- **1 porcini mushroom, diced**
- **½ tsp dried basil**
- **½ tsp dried oregano**
- **juice of 2 limes**
- **1 tbsp fresh parsley, finely chopped**
- **2 spring onions, cleaned and finely sliced**
- **1 clove of garlic, peeled and diced**
- **25g reduced fat cheese, finely grated**
- **salt and black pepper**
- **rapeseed oil spray**
- **a few mint leaves to serve (optional)**

1. Bring a large saucepan of water to the boil.

2. Using a sharp knife carefully cut off about 1 inch from the top of the artichoke, and a thin slice off the bottom to form an even base.

3. Remove any very tough outer leaves and discard them. Trim off the sharp tips of the leaves with a pair of kitchen scissors.

4. Carefully pull the leaves away from the middle of the artichoke, only a few so that you can see down to the choke. Using a spoon gently scrape away and discard all of the fuzz, to reveal a clean heart. Once done drizzle a little of the lime juice inside to help prevent discolouration.

5. Place the artichoke in the boiling water and cook for about 10-15 minutes. To check if it is ready pull off an outer leaf - It should come away easily. Remove from the water and set aside to drain.

6. Preheat the oven to 190°C, 375°F, Gas Mark 5.

7. Heat a small frying pan and add a couple of sprays of the rapeseed oil. Add the garlic and spring onions and cook for 2-3 minutes. Add the remaining lime juice, dried basil, oregano, porcini mushroom and white wine to the garlic and spring onion mixture. Stir and cook for a further 3 minutes on a low heat.

8. Add the breadcrumbs and parsley, stir to combine and remove from the heat. Season to taste with salt and pepper and set aside to cool.

9. Place the artichoke in a small ovenproof dish base side down. Carefully fill the artichoke with the stuffing mixture. Sprinkle over the finely grated cheese.

10. Place in the oven and cook for 15 minutes.

11. Remove from the oven and serve hot garnished with mint leaves (optional).

Meat Free Shakshuka

per serving:
Calories 437, Fat 23g, Sugar 27g, Salt 1.6g
Prep time: 5 minutes
Cook time: 25-30 minutes

- **1 x 200g can of chopped tomatoes**
- **2 duck eggs (or 2 large hen's eggs)**
- **1 small white onion, peeled and sliced**
- **1 small red onion peeled and sliced**
- **1 small red pepper, deseeded and diced**
- **1 small orange pepper, deseeded and diced**
- **1 small yellow pepper, deseeded and diced**
- **1 small clove of garlic, peeled and finely diced**
- **½ tsp smoked paprika**
- **½ tsp cumin seeds**
- **pinch cayenne pepper powder**
- **1 tbsp tomato puree**
- **50ml vegetable stock**
- **1 tbsp of fresh coriander leaves, chopped**
- **salt and freshly ground black pepper**
- **rapeseed oil spray**

1. Heat a frying pan and spray with a little rapeseed oil. Add the onions and peppers. Cook until the peppers and onions have started to soften.

2. Add garlic and cook for a further 2 minutes, then add the cumin seeds and the paprika and cayenne into the frying pan. Stir in the tomato puree and cook for 3-4 minutes. Add the chopped tomatoes and the vegetable stock.

3. Reduce the heat to a simmer and cook for a further 5-10 minutes until the sauce has thickened but is not dry, then stir in the chopped coriander and season with salt and black pepper.

4. Make two wells in the tomato mixture and crack an egg into each well. If you have a lid for the frying pan then place it on top, if not then take a large piece of foil and place it shiny side down gently on the top of the frying pan taking care not to touch the eggs. Cook for 3-4 minutes. Remove the lid or foil and serve straight away. Garnish with fresh coriander or parsley.

TIP
Don't overcook the duck eggs as they will go rubbery.

Courgette Soup

per serving:
Calories 96, Fat 4.2g, Sugar 7.2g, Salt 1.3g
Prep time: 5 minutes
Cook time: 25 minutes

- **350g courgettes, diced into 1cm cubes**
- **sea salt and white pepper, to season**
- **150ml vegetable stock**
- **rapeseed oil spray**
- **¼ tsp tsps garlic paste**
- **2 spring onions, cleaned, root removed and rough chopped**
- **1 tbsp low-fat plain yoghurt, optional**

1. Heat a heavy-based saucepan over a medium heat and add a couple of sprays of the rapeseed oil.

2. Add the chopped spring onions, garlic paste, and diced courgettes - cook for 10-15 minutes until slightly browned.

3. Add the stock and allow to simmer for 10 minutes. Remove from the heat and then pour the mixture into a blender and blend until smooth.

4. Season with a little salt and white pepper, pour into a warmed bowl and swirl in the yoghurt is using. Serve straight away

Creamy Mushrooms
with Spaghetti

per serving:
Calories 323, Fat 12g, Sugar 5.8g, Salt 0.6g
Prep time: 5 minutes
Cook time: 15 minutes

- **140g chestnut mushrooms, cleaned and sliced**
- **50g (dry weight) spaghetti**
- **60g light cream cheese**
- **1 tbsp milk**
- **rapeseed oil spray**

1. Bring a pan of water to the boil and add the spaghetti. Cook for 10 minutes.

2. While the spaghetti is cooking, preheat a small frying pan and a couple of sprays of rapeseed oil. Add the sliced mushrooms and cook for 4-5 minutes or until softened.

3. Reduce the heat and add the cream cheese followed by the milk, stir continuously until the sauce is smooth and keep warm.

4. Once the spaghetti is cooked drain and return to the saucepan. Add the creamy mushroom mixture and stir gently to evenly coat the pasta.

5. Serve in a warm pasta dish.

Spicy Tofu and Quinoa Stir-fry

per serving:
Calories 554, Fat 16.5g, Sugar 15.2g, Salt 0.9g
Prep time: 5 minutes
Cook time: 25-30 minutes

- **245g cooked quinoa**
- **100g cauliflower florets**
- **100g broccoli florets**
- **150g firm tofu**
- **2 tsps honey or golden syrup**
- **1 spring onion, cleaned, root removed and sliced**
- **5g toasted flaked almonds**
- **¼ tsp tsps sesame seeds**
- **1 tbsp rice wine vinegar**
- **½ tsp tsps dry chilli flakes or 1 small red chilli, deseeded and finely diced**
- **3 tsps gluten free soy sauce**
- **fresh parsley, to serve (optional)**

1. Preheat oven to 200°C, 400°F, gas Mark 6.

2. Cut the tofu into 2cm cubes. Place in a bowl, add the chilli flakes or fresh chilli and 1 tsp Honea and 1 tsp of soy sauce. Gently stir until the tofu is coated in the spice mix. Place on a baking sheet and bake for 20-25 minutes, until tofu has crisped up - keep an eye on it so that it does not burn, turning occasionally.

3. While tofu is baking, heat a pan of water until boiling then add the broccoli and cauliflower florets. Cook for 3-4 minutes, then drain and set aside.

4. In a small bowl mix together the remaining soy sauce, rice wine vinegar, sliced spring onion and honey.

5. Once the tofu is cooked, heat a frying pan over medium-high heat. Add the broccoli, cauliflower, tofu and quinoa and cook for 2-3 minutes until warm. Add sauce, toss to coat and cook for another 1-2 minutes. Add sesame seeds and stir, then serve straightaway.

6. To serve place in a warmed bowl and sprinkle over the toasted flaked almonds and a little fresh parsley (optional).

Sweet Potato Soup

per serving:
Calories 192, Fat 2.8g, Sugar 12g, Salt 2.5g
Prep time: 5 minutes
Cook time: 10 minutes (not including pre baking the potato)

- **1 medium sweet potato (approx. 200g raw weight) – oven baked in its skin and cooled**
- **200ml vegetable stock**
- **1 small shallot, peeled and sliced**
- **pinch of sea salt**
- **1 small clove of garlic, peeled and diced**
- **½ tsp ground cumin**
- **freshly ground black pepper to taste**
- **1 tsp fresh parsley or coriander (optional)**
- **rapeseed oil spray**

1. Cut the cooled baked sweet potato in half and scoop out the soft flesh into a saucepan, discarding the skin (see tip below).

2. Heat a frying pan, add a couple of sprays of the oil and then add the shallot and garlic and cook on a medium heat for 2-3 minutes. Add the salt and cumin and cook for a further minute.

3. Pour 150ml of the stock into the saucepan with the sweet potato and slowly bring to the boil.

4. Whilst this is happening take the frying pan off the heat and gently add the remaining stock. Stir to release everything from the bottom of the pan. Gently pour the ingredients into the saucepan with the sweet potato and stock.

5. Bring to the boil, and then reduce to a simmer for 5 minutes.

6. Once cooked, allow to cool slightly before blending the soup until smooth. Season to taste with the black pepper.

7. Reheat if necessary and serve with the fresh herbs sprinkled over the top if required.

TIP

Rather than discard the skin, flatten it out onto a non-stick baking tray, spray with a little rapeseed oil and season with salt. Bake in a hot oven until crispy. Eat as a snack.

Chunky Vegetable Dhal

per serving:
Calories 291, Fat 5.1g, Sugar 18g, Salt 1.6g
Prep time: 5 minutes
Cook time: 55-60 minutes

- **150g cauliflower, broken into small florets**
- **1 small sweet potato, peeled and cubed**
- **1 small carrot, peeled and cubed**
- **20g baby spinach**
- **30g dry red lentils**
- **1 small white onion, peeled and chopped**
- **250ml hot vegetable stock**
- **1 tsp turmeric**
- **1 ½ tbsps garam masala**
- **1 tsp ground cumin**
- **½ green chilli, deseeded and diced**
- **pinch of salt and black pepper**
- **rapeseed oil spray**

1. Preheat the oven to 200°C, 400°F, Gas Mark 6.

2. Place the cauliflower, sweet potato, carrot and onion into a small ovenproof dish, spray with a little rapeseed oil and season with salt and pepper. Place in the oven for about 15-20 minutes until beginning to brown.

3. Remove from the oven and turn the oven heat down to 185°C, 375°F, Gas Mark 5.

4. Add the red lentils, spinach, garam masala, turmeric, cumin and chilli to the hot stock and stir to combine. Carefully pour over the cooked vegetables in the hot ovenproof dish and stir so that nothing has stuck to the bottom.

5. Cover the dish with foil (shiny side down) and place back into the oven. Cook for a further 25-30 minutes or until the lentils are cooked and the liquid has been absorbed.

6. Serve piping hot.

Pumpkin and Rosemary Risotto

per serving:
Calories 290, Fat 4.1g, Sugar 3.2g, Salt 1.3g
Prep time: 10 minutes
Cook time: 25-30 minutes

- **180g pumpkin flesh, cut into 2cm chunks**
- **55g (dry weight) arborio risotto rice**
- **220ml hot vegetable stock**
- **50ml dry white wine**
- **½ tsp dried rosemary**
- **1 garlic clove, peeled and finely chopped**
- **salt and freshly ground black pepper to taste**
- **rapeseed oil spray**

1. Preheat the oven to 200°C, 400°F, Gas Mark 6.

2. Place the pumpkin chunks on a non-stick baking tray and spray with the rapeseed oil spray. Roast for 15 minutes until just soft.

3. Meanwhile, in a non-stick pan, cook the garlic for 1 minute then add the rice and rosemary and gradually stir in a third of the stock and all of the wine. Allow the rice to absorb the liquid before adding the remaining stock, a third at a time (this will take between 15-20 minutes).

4. Once all the liquid has been added, stir in the roasted pumpkin, cover and continue to cook for a further 2-3 minutes. Remove from the heat and season with the salt and black pepper if required.

5. Serve the risotto in a warmed pasta bowl.

Mushroom and Gnocchi Medley

per serving:
Calories 423, Fat 4.4g, Sugar 3g, Salt 1.4g
Prep time: 5 minutes
Cook time: 10-15 minutes

- 180g fresh gnocchi
- 100g chestnut mushrooms, sliced
- 40g shitake
- 40g porcini
- 70ml dry white wine
- 1 garlic clove, peeled and diced
- a little parmesan cheese
- 1 vegetable stock cube
- fresh parsley for serving
- rapeseed oil spray

1. Bring a large pan of water to the boil and add the stock cube. Add the gnocchi and cook for 1-2 minutes, then drain and set aside.

2. In the meantime preheat a frying pan and add a couple of sprays of the rapeseed oil. Add the garlic and mushrooms and gently fry for 3-4 minutes, then add the wine and cook until it has reduced right down.

3. Add the gnocchi and gently stir to combine, being careful not to mash the gnocchi. Cook for a further 1-2 minutes.

4. Transfer to a warm plate and top with the fresh parsley and grated parmesan.

Cream of Mushroom and Tarragon Soup

per serving:
Calories 122, Fat 4.6g, Sugar 11g, Salt 0.6g
Prep time: 5 minutes
Cook time: 20 minutes

- 100ml whole milk
- 150ml vegetable stock
- 40g chestnut mushrooms, sliced
- 2 Portobello mushrooms, sliced
- 1 small white onion, peeled and diced
- ¼ tsp dried tarragon
- freshly ground black pepper
- 1 tsp cornflour

1. In a non-stick pan dry-fry the onion until soft then add the mushrooms and cook for a further 3-4 minutes. Remove a couple of the sliced mushrooms and reserve for garnish. Add the tarragon and milk. Mix the cornflour with a little of the stock then whisk into the pan.

2. Continue to stir allowing the soup to thicken before gradually stirring in the remaining stock. Simmer gently for 15 minutes.

3. Remove from the heat and using a blender, blitz the soup until smooth. Season with the black pepper.

4. Pour into a warmed soup bowl and top with the reserved mushroom slices and a little freshly ground black pepper.

Sweet Potato and Okra Stew

per serving:
Calories 258, Fat 5.6g, Sugar 20g, Salt 1.1g
Prep time: 5 minutes
Cook time: 25-30 minutes

- 150g sweet potato, peeled and cut into 1cm cubes
- 90g fresh okra, top and tailed and chopped into 1.5cm slices
- 150ml vegetable stock
- 50g tomato passata
- 1 small white onion, peeled and sliced
- 6 cherry tomatoes, halved
- 1 small red chilli, deseeded and chopped finely
- 1 tsp garam masala
- ½ tsp turmeric
- rapeseed oil spray
- fresh parsley leaves, optional

1.Heat a heavy based frying pan and add a couple of sprays of the oil. Now add the onion, sweet potato and the red chilli and cook for 3-5 minutes, stirring occasionally.

2. Add the vegetable stock, garam masala, turmeric and tomato passata and cook for a further 10 minutes on a medium heat until the potato chunks are just starting to soften. Add the okra and the cherry tomatoes and simmer for a further 10-12 minutes until the sauce has reduced right away.

3. Serve straight away, garnish with a few fresh parsley leaves (optional).

Avocado, Orange and Radish Shells

per serving:
Calories 285, Fat 27g, Sugar 6.1g, Salt 1g
Prep time: 5 minutes

- 1 small avocado
- 1 small orange, peeled and cut into segments
- 4 radishes
- ½ baby gem lettuce, shredded
- uice of 1 lime
- pinch of salt

1. Cut the avocado in half and carefully remove the stone. Using a spoon carefully scoop out the flesh into a bowl ensuring you don't damage the shell/skin of the avocado.

2. Set the shell aside, but do not discard. Roughly chop the avocado flesh and add the lime juice and a pinch of salt. Gently stir to cover the avocado in the juice.

3. Add the lettuce, orange segments, chopped radishes to the avocado and lime mixture, stir to combine and then divide equally between the two avocado shells. Serve straightaway.

Mushroom, Courgette and Chickpea Stir-fry

per serving:
Calories 244, Fat 4.2g, Sugar 18.1g, Salt 1.5g
Prep time: 5 minutes
Cook time: 20 minutes

- **120g chickpeas (drained weight)**
- **125g button mushrooms, cleaned and cut in half**
- **1 medium courgette, halved and sliced**
- **1½ tsps dark soy sauce or gluten free soy sauce**
- **1 tsp muscovado dark brown sugar**
- **freshly ground black pepper**
- **1 handful fresh coriander**
- **1 small red chilli, deseeded and finely diced**
- **rapeseed oil spray**

1. Heat a frying pan over medium heat and add a couple of sprays of the rapeseed oil. Add the chickpeas, chilli and courgette and cook for 10 minutes, stirring occasionally.

2. Stir in mushrooms, soy sauce, muscovado sugar and coriander, and cook until tender, stirring occasionally. Season with a little black pepper and serve immediately.

Sides &
sauces

Simple Sweet Chilli Sauce

per serving:
Calories 45, Fat 0g, Sugar 11g, Salt 0.1g
Prep time: 5 minutes
Cook time: 5-10 minutes

- 200ml water
- 20ml white wine vinegar
- 100g caster sugar
- 2 small red chillies, top removed and cut into two pieces, do not deseed
- pinch of sea salt

1. Put all of the ingredients into a small heavy based saucepan, and bring to the boil over a high heat, stirring occasionally, and cook for 5-10 minutes until the liquid has reduced by a third.

2. Remove from the heat and allow to cool. Pour the cooled liquid into a blender and blitz until the chillies have been cut into small pieces. Pour into a jar. Store in the fridge until required.

Quick Tomato Salsa

per serving:
Calories 26, Fat 0g, Sugar 4g, Salt 1g
Prep time: 5 minutes

- 120g very ripe fresh tomatoes, deseeded
- 1 spring onion, cleaned and roughly chopped
- 1 tbsp fresh coriander, roughly chopped
- 1 small clove of garlic, peeled
- pinch of salt
- ½ small green chilli

1. Place all of the ingredients into a blender and blend for 10-20 seconds or until the desired texture is obtained.

2. Leave in the fridge for at least 1 hour to get the best flavour.

3. Serve straightaway or keep in the fridge for up to 2 days.

Simple Chilli Jam

per serving:
Calories 46, Fat 0g, Sugar 11g, Salt 0.15g
Prep time: 5 minutes
Cook time: 40 minutes

- **1 x 200g can of chopped tomatoes**
- **75g dark muscovado sugar**
- **1 small red onion, peeled and quartered**
- **2 red chillies**
- **1 tbsp balsamic vinegar**
- **rapeseed oil spray**
- **a pinch of sea salt and black pepper to taste**

1. Remove the tops from both the chillies and place in a blender with the onion and blend until very finely chopped.

2. Heat a small heavy based frying pan until hot. Add a couple of sprays of the rapeseed oil and add the onion and chilli mixture to the pan and cook for 2-3 minutes until softened – stirring all the time.

3. Add the balsamic vinegar to the pan and cook for a further minute.

4. Add the sugar, stir until fully mixed in. Cook until the mixture starts to boil, turn the heat down slightly to control the boiling, cook for a further 5 minutes, then add the salt and a little black pepper.

5. Gently pour in the chopped tomatoes and stir. Bring back to the boil then reduce the heat to achieve a simmer. Cook for a further 30 minutes or until the excess liquid has been absorbed and a thick consistency has been achieved.

6. Allow to cool completely then store in the fridge in an airtight container – this will keep for 7 days.

7. This is great with a burger, in a cheese sandwich, as a pizza topping, a quick pasta sauce (thin it down with a tiny amount of hot water) and so much more!

Roasted Pumpkin Wedges

with Feta and Mint

per serving:
Calories 109, Fat 6.2g, Sugar 3.6g, Salt 1.2g
Prep time: 5 minutes
Cook time: 40 minutes

- **150g pumpkin, peeled, seeds discarded and cut into 1 cm thick wedges**
- **20g reduced fat feta cheese**
- **rapeseed oil spray**
- **salt and freshly ground black pepper**
- **1 sprig of fresh mint, roughly chopped**

1. Preheat the oven to 210°C, 410°F, Gas mark 7 or the top oven in an Aga or similar. Place some baking parchment on a baking sheet. Arrange the pumpkin wedges on the baking parchment. Lightly spray with the rapeseed oil and dust with a little salt and freshly ground black pepper. Place in the oven on a high shelf.

2. After 20 minutes, remove the pumpkin from the oven. Sprinkle over the crumbled feta cheese and return to the oven for a further 5 minutes.

3. Remove from the oven, transfer to a bowl and sprinkle over the fresh mint and serve straightaway.

Barbecue Sauce

per serving;
Calories 51, Fat 0g, Sugar 12g, Salt 0.4g
Prep time: 2 minutes
Cook time: 25 minutes

- **120g passata**
- **50g dark muscovado sugar**
- **1 tbsp Worcestershire sauce**
- **¼ tsp black pepper**
- **1 tbsp balsamic vinegar**
- **pinch of sea salt**

1. Place all of the ingredients into a small heavy based saucepan.

2. Gently bring to the boil then reduce the heat to a simmer, stirring occasionally, and cook for 25 minutes.

3. Remove from the heat and allow to cool. Pour into a glass jar and store in the fridge for 7-10 days.

Marie Rose Sauce

per serving;
Calories 44, Fat 1.8g, Sugar 4.5g, Salt 0.8g
Prep time: 5 minutes

- **2 tbsp extra light mayonnaise**
- **½ tsp Worcestershire sauce**
- **juice of half a lime**
- **1 tsp tomato ketchup**
- **2 drops of Tabasco sauce**
- **pinch smoked paprika**

1. Place all of the ingredients into a small bowl. Mix together and use straightaway or store in the fridge for 24 hours.

TIP
Great with shellfish such as cold cooked prawns or with crab sticks.

Celeriac Remoulade

per serving:
Calories 67, Fat 2.8g, Sugar 4.7g, Salt 1.5g
Prep time: 5 minutes

- **150g celeriac**
- **2 tsp Dijon mustard**
- **1½ tbsps extra light mayonnaise**
- **juice from 1 lime**
- **freshly ground black pepper**

1. Place the mustard, mayonnaise, lime juice and a little black pepper in a bowl and mix until combined.

2. Remove the outer layer of the celeriac and coarsely grate into the sauce bowl. Stir until coated.

3. This will keep for 24 hours in the fridge.

Red and White Slaw

per serving:
Calories 26, Fat 0g, Sugar 4g, Salt 1g
Prep time: 5 minutes

- **75g red cabbage**
- **1 small fennel bulb**
- **1 tsp Dijon mustard**
- **1 tbsp extra light mayonnaise**
- **juice from 1 lime**
- **freshly ground black pepper**

1. Place the mustard, mayonnaise, lime juice and a little black pepper in a bowl and mix until combined.

2. Shred the red cabbage and add to the mixture.

3. Remove the tufts from the top of the fennel and reserve. Cut the base off the fennel and discard. Shred the fennel bulb and add to the mixture.

4. Take about a teaspoon of the fennel tufts and roughly chop and add to the bowl. Mix everything together, and season with a little more black pepper if required.

5. This will keep for 24 hours in the fridge.

Cucumber and Parsley Coleslaw

per serving:
Calories 25, Fat 0.5g, Sugar 3.7g, Salt 0.52g
Prep time: 5 minutes

- **65g white cabbage, finely shredded**
- **40g cucumber, cut into small sticks**
- **10g (small handful) fresh parsley, roughly chopped**
- **salt and freshly ground black pepper**

1. Place all of the ingredients into a non-metallic bowl. Stir to combine then season with a little salt and black pepper.

TIP
For a zingy flavour, swap the cucumber for a pickled gherkin.

Mushroom Rice

per serving:
Calories 213, Fat 1.5g, Sugar 1.3g, Salt 0.2g
Prep time: 5 minutes
Cook time: 20 minutes

- **55g (dry weight) basmati rice**
- **80g button mushrooms, sliced**
- **1 tsp Worcestershire sauce**
- **black pepper**
- **rapeseed oil spray**
- **a few parsley leaves (optional)**

1. Bring a pan of water to the boil and add the rice.

2. In the meantime, heat a small frying pan, add a couple of sprays of the rapeseed oil and then add the mushrooms, Worcestershire sauce and a little black pepper and cook for 4-5 minutes until softened. Remove from the heat and set aside.

3. Drain the rice as soon as it is cooked and transfer it to the pan with the mushrooms in it. Stir gently to combine, season with a little black pepper and transfer the mushroom rice to a warmed bowl.

4. Sprinkle with a little fresh parsley (optional).

TIP
This rice is great with grilled beef steak or salmon.

Cauliflower Rice

per serving;
Calories 54, Fat 0.9g, Sugar 5g, Salt 0.46g
Prep time: 2-3 minutes
Cook time: 1 minute

- **180g cauliflower florets**
- **1 vegetable stock cube**

1. Boil 600ml of water in a saucepan, adding the vegetable stock cube.

2. Break the cauliflower into florets and blend in a food processor until they form the consistency of breadcrumbs. Add this cauliflower 'rice' to the boiling water for 30 seconds, then drain well through a sieve before serving.

Egg Fried Rice

per serving:
Calories 286, Fat 6.8g, Sugar 5g, Salt 0.2g
Prep time: 5 minutes
Cook time: 20 minutes

- **45g (dry weight) basmati rice**
- **25g frozen peas**
- **25g frozen sweetcorn**
- **½ small onion, peeled and diced**
- **1 small egg, beaten**
- **rapeseed oil**

1. Cook the rice in a pan of boiling water. Two minutes before the rice is cooked add the peas and sweetcorn, cook for two more minutes then drain.

2. Heat a non-stick frying pan and add a couple of sprays of the rapeseed oil. Add the onion and cook for 2-3 minutes. Add the rice/pea/sweetcorn mixture, stir and cook for a further 1-2 minutes.

3. Move the rice to the edge of the pan and add another spray of oil to the visible pan area, pour in the egg, leave for 10 seconds then mix quickly into the rice mixture until the rice is coated.

4. Serve straightaway.

Chorizo Hasselback Baked Potato

per serving:
Calories 300, Fat 13g, Sugar 2.4g, Salt 1.6g
Prep time: 5 minutes
Cook time: 80 minutes

- **1 baking potato (approx. 180g)**
- **30g reduced fat chorizo**
- **20g reduced fat cheese, grated**
- **1 garlic clove, cut in half**
- **rapeseed oil**

TIP
Cut a thin layer off the base of the potato before your start to stop it wobbling, then place wooden spoons either side of the potato so you don't cut all the way through.

1. Preheat the oven to 200°C, 400°F, Gas Mark 6.

2. Peel the potato and rub the outside with the cut garlic clove (discard the garlic).

3. Cut slices into the potato 3mm apart and about 8mm from the bottom. Place on a baking tray.

4. Spray with a little rapeseed oil and place in the top part of the oven.

5. After 45 minutes remove the potato from the oven . Cut the chorizo into thin slices and place a slice in between each opening. Return to the oven for a further 15 minutes then remove again and sprinkle with the grated cheese. Return to the oven and cook for a further 10 minutes or until the cheese is melted.

Basic Tomato Pasta Sauce

per serving:
Calories 65, Fat 0g, Sugar 9.3g, Salt 0.2g
Prep time: 3 minutes
Cook time: 5 minutes

- **1 x 200g can of chopped tomatoes**
- **2 tsps tomato puree**
- **1 tsp Italian mixed herbs**
- **freshly ground black pepper**
- **dash of Worcestershire sauce (optional)**

1. Place all of the ingredients in a blender and blitz for 30 seconds.

2. Place in a small saucepan, bring to the boil, then reduce to a simmer for 2 minutes. Serve with pasta.

TIPS -
If using in a Bolognese or lasagne then there is no need to cook it separately.
Double up on the tomato puree and this makes a great pizza topping. There is no need to cook before using.

Zingy Raita

per serving:
Calories 46, Fat 0g, Sugar 6.7g, Salt 1g
Prep time: 5 minutes

- **3 tbsps low-fat plain yoghurt**
- **1 small pickled gherkin, finely diced**
- **1 spring onion, cleaned and finely sliced – keep about 2cm of the dark green part for a garnish**
- **¼ tsp mint sauce**

1. Place all of the ingredients into a small bowl, mix together and either use straight away or store in the fridge for up to 24 hours.

2. Garnish with the remaining sliced spring onion tops.

TIP
Great with curry or cold meats.
Swap the pickled gherkin for a baby cucumber.

Whole Roasted Cauliflower
with Parsley and Parmesan

per serving:
Calories 142, Fat 7.5g, Sugar 7.6g, Salt 1.2g
Prep time: 5 minutes
Cook time: 30 minutes

- **1 x 265g small whole cauliflower**
- **10g parmesan cheese, finely grated**
- **1 tbsp fresh parsley, finely chopped**
- **rapeseed oil spray**
- **juice of 1 lime**
- **½ tsp turmeric**
- **½ tsp ground coriander**
- **½ tsp ground cumin**
- **½ tsp garlic paste or 1 small garlic clove, peeled and finely diced**
- **freshly ground black pepper**
- **sea salt**

1. Preheat the oven to 180°C, 350°F, Gas Mark 4.

2. Place the lime juice, garlic paste, ground cumin, turmeric, ground coriander, salt and a little black pepper in a small bowl and mix together to make a paste.

3. Cut the base of the cauliflower to help remove any green leaves and remove the hard stem.

4. Evenly coat the whole cauliflower with the paste mix. Place on a non-stick baking tray and spray with just a couple of squirts of the rapeseed oil. Place in the oven and bake for 30 minutes or until golden in colour.

5. Remove from the oven and transfer to a warmed serving plate, sprinkle with the chopped parsley and the grated cheese and serve straightaway.

Index